AF669611

Finance Gita 50

Composed By: Sachin H Hulageri, Bengaluru, India
Published By: Gayitri S Hulageri, Bengaluru, India
ISBN : 978-93-5810-605-3
Contact Us: Gita365.forever@gmail.com

Preface

Handle Finance Emotion – The Gita Way

A practical and thought-provoking handbook for professionals and business owners, Handle Finance Emotions – The Gita Way helps readers navigate everyday financial emotions using the timeless wisdom of the Bhagavad Gita.

Designed as a quick reference guide, the book explores 50 common financial emotions and situations, thoughtfully organized into five key areas: Spending, Saving & Financial Security, Debt & Liability Management, Investment & Behavior, and Wealth Creation.

Each topic follows a clear and structured format—presenting a relevant Gita shloka, a simple translation, its deeper meaning, and practical actions that can be applied in real-life financial decisions.

To enhance understanding and relatability, every emotion is brought to life through visual illustrations and short stories, making complex financial behaviors easier to reflect upon and manage.

Blending ancient philosophy with modern financial challenges, this handbook offers a calm, balanced, and disciplined approach to money—helping readers make wiser decisions with clarity and emotional stability.

|| Shri Krishnarpanamastu ||

Index

Index

SPENDING
SP01 : Overspending

Shloka 6.16	*nātyaśhnatastu yogo 'sti* *na chaikāntam anaśhnataḥ* *na chāti-svapna-śhīlasya* *jāgrato naiva chārjuna*
Simple Translation	• Neither excess nor extreme denial brings balance. • Moderation is the path to stability.
Meaning	• Financial discipline requires self-control. • Balanced habits prevent regret and stress.
Actions	• Create a realistic monthly budget. • Track and review expenses daily.

1

SPENDING
SP01 : Overspending

Balance in Spending

Troubled by overspending, she reflected on moderation. Creating a monthly budget and tracking expenses daily, awareness replaced impulse. Gradually, discipline grew, teaching her that financial peace emerges not from deprivation or excess, but from mindful balance and conscious choices aligned with long-term wellbeing.

S1

SPENDING
SP02 : Living Paycheck to Paycheck

Shloka 3.8	***niyataṁ kuru karma tvaṁ karma jyāyo hyakarmaṇaḥ śharīra-yātrāpi cha te na prasiddhyed akarmaṇaḥ***
Simple Translation	• **Perform your necessary duties.** • **Action is better than inaction.**
Meaning	• **Financial stability needs discipline.** • **Responsibility builds security.**
Actions	• **Follow a fixed savings rule every month.** • **Reduce non-essential spending consistently.**

2

SPENDING
SP02 : Living Paycheck to Paycheck

Growth Through Steady Steps

Living paycheck to paycheck, he stopped postponing responsibility. Setting a simple savings rule and cutting unnecessary expenses, structure entered his finances. Small actions compounded, teaching him that financial stability grows when disciplined effort replaces delay and mindful choices guide everyday spending.

S2

SPENDING
SP03 : Impulsive Purchases

Shloka 2.63	***krodhād bhavati sammohaḥ sammohāt smṛiti-vibhramaḥ smṛiti-bhranśhād buddhi-nāśho buddhi-nāśhāt praṇaśhyati***
Simple Translation	• **From uncontrolled desire comes confusion.** • **From confusion, judgment is lost.**
Meaning	• **Impulse clouds financial wisdom.** • **Self-control protects your resources.**
Actions	• **Pause 24 hours before non-essential purchases.** • **Differentiate clearly between need and want.**

3

SPENDING
SP03 : Impulsive Purchases

The Pause That Protects Wealth

Driven by impulse, she often bought without thinking. Remembering how desire clouds judgment, she practiced waiting twenty-four hours before purchases. By separating needs from wants, clarity returned, teaching her that a small pause can save money, protect wisdom, and restore control over impulsive habits.

S3

SPENDING
SP04 : Poor Money Management

Shloka 6.17	***yuktāhāra-vihārasya yukta-cheṣhṭasya karmasu yukta-svapnāvabodhasya yogo bhavati duḥkha-hā***
Simple Translation	• **Balance in habits brings well-being.** • **Moderation removes distress.**
Meaning	• **Money management requires discipline.** • **Balanced spending creates stability.**
Actions	• **Review and track your monthly budget.** • **Allocate income intentionally across needs and goals.**

4

SPENDING
SP04 : Poor Money Management

Discipline in Financial Living

Poor money management left him anxious and reactive. Embracing balanced habits, he tracked a monthly budget and allocated funds with intention. Order replaced chaos, teaching him that financial wellbeing grows from disciplined routines, conscious choices, and steady alignment between income, expenses, and priorities.

S4

SPENDING
SP05 : Living Beyond Means

Shloka 16.21	***tri-vidhaṁ narakasyedaṁ dvāraṁ nāśhanam ātmanaḥ kāmaḥ krodhastathā lobhas tasmād etat trayaṁ tyajet***
Simple Translation	• **Desire, anger, and greed lead to ruin.** • **Avoid these paths to protect yourself.**
Meaning	• **Unchecked desire causes financial strain.** • **Simple living preserves long-term stability.**
Actions	• **Avoid lifestyle comparison and impulse upgrades.** • **Spend consciously within your real income.**

05

SPENDING
SP05 : Living Beyond Means

Freedom Through Simplicity

Living beyond her means, she chased comparisons and appearances. Recognizing desire as the trap, she chose conscious simplicity. Letting go of lifestyle inflation, peace returned, teaching her that true wealth grows when wants are restrained and life is shaped by values, not constant comparison.

S5

SPENDING
SP06 : Not Tracking Expenses

Shloka 4.7	***yadā yadā hi dharmasya glānir bhavati bhārata abhyutthānam adharmasya tadātmānaṁ sṛijāmyaham***
Simple Translation	• **Whenever imbalance arises,** • **Restoration begins with awareness.**
Meaning	• **Financial order starts with clarity.** • **Awareness creates control.**
Actions	• **Track your expenses every week.** • **Categorize spending to identify patterns.**

6

SPENDING
SP06 : Not Tracking Expenses

Awareness Restores Order

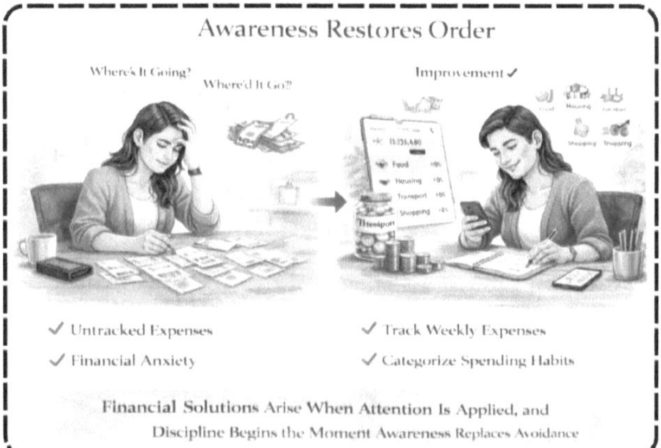

Money kept slipping away unnoticed, creating quiet anxiety. Choosing awareness, she began tracking expenses weekly and categorizing spending patterns. Clarity emerged. Control returned gently, teaching her that financial solutions arise when attention is applied, and discipline begins the moment awareness replaces avoidance.

S6

SPENDING
SP07 : Overspending on Lifestyle Upgrades

Shloka 16.21	***tri-vidhaṁ narakasyedaṁ dvāraṁ nāśhanam ātmanaḥ kāmaḥ krodhastathā lobhas tasmād etat trayaṁ tyajet***
Simple Translation	• **Desire, anger, and greed lead to downfall.** • **Avoid these to protect yourself.**
Meaning	• **Lifestyle inflation weakens savings.** • **Contentment strengthens financial freedom.**
Actions	• **Restrict unnecessary lifestyle upgrades.** • **Practice conscious and simple living.**

7

SPENDING
SP07 : Overspending on Lifestyle Upgrades

Choosing Simplicity Over Show

Chasing constant lifestyle upgrades, he watched savings shrink. Recognizing desire as the trap, he limited non-essential purchases and embraced simple living. Contentment replaced comparison, teaching him that lasting financial freedom grows when wants are restrained and life is guided by values, not display.

S7

SPENDING
SP08 : Lack of Budgeting Discipline

Shloka 6.17	***yuktāhāra-vihārasya yukta-cheṣhṭasya karmasu yukta-svapnāvabodhasya yogo bhavati duḥkha-hā***
Simple Translation	• **Moderation in habits brings well-being.** • **Balanced living removes distress.**
Meaning	• **Budgeting creates financial balance.** • **Discipline prevents money stress.**
Actions	• **Apply the 50-30-20 budgeting rule.** • **Review and adjust spending weekly.**

8

SPENDING
SP08 : Lack of Budgeting Discipline

Harmony Through Budgeted Living

Lacking budgeting discipline, his finances felt chaotic and stressful. Embracing balance, he followed the 50-30-20 rule and reviewed spending weekly. Gradually, harmony returned, teaching him that financial wellbeing is sustained when moderation, awareness, and regular reflection guide everyday money choices.

S8

SPENDING

SP09 : Buying Unnecessary Luxury Items

Shloka 3.39	***āvṛitaṁ jñānam etena jñānino nitya-vairiṇā kāma-rūpeṇa kaunteya duṣhpūreṇānalena cha***
Simple Translation	• **Desire veils true wisdom.** • **It burns like an endless fire.**
Meaning	• **Impulse weakens financial judgment.** • **Luxury must be intentional, not emotional.**
Actions	• **Adopt a 30-day waiting rule before buying.** • **Purchase only if the need remains genuine.**

9

SPENDING
SP09 : Buying Unnecessary Luxury Items

Wisdom Over Want

Tempted by luxury, he often mistook desire for need. Remembering how craving clouds wisdom, he adopted a thirty-day pause before buying. Time revealed truth. Many urges faded, teaching him that planned choices preserve wealth, clarity, and dignity far better than impulsive indulgence ever could.

S9

SPENDING
SP10 : Difficulty Controlling Cash Flow

Shloka 6.16	***nātyaśhnatastu yogo 'sti na chaikāntam anaśhnataḥ na chāti-svapna-śhīlasya jāgrato naiva chārjuna***
Simple Translation	• **Neither excess nor neglect brings balance.** • **Moderation leads to stability.**
Meaning	• **Uncontrolled spending disrupts cash flow.** • **Balanced habits create financial steadiness.**
Actions	• **Monitor monthly income and expenses carefully.** • **Cut down discretionary spending consistently.**

10

SPENDING
SP10 : Difficulty Controlling Cash Flow

Stability Through Moderation

Uncontrolled cash flow created constant stress. Embracing moderation, he tracked monthly income and expenses, reducing discretionary spending. Gradually, balance returned, teaching him that financial stability is sustained not by earning more alone, but by conscious control and measured use of resources.

S10

SAVINGS & FINANCIAL SECURITY
SS 01 : No Savings Habit

Shloka **2.47**	***karmaṇy-evādhikāras te mā phaleṣhu kadāchana mā karma-phala-hetur bhūr mā te saṅgo 'stvakarmaṇi***
Simple Translation	• **You have control over your actions.** • **Do not depend on immediate results.**
Meaning	• **Wealth grows through steady discipline.** • **Consistency matters more than amount.**
Actions	• **Automate a fixed monthly savings transfer.** • **Begin immediately—even with a small sum.**

11

SAVINGS & FINANCIAL SECURITY
SS 01 : No Savings Habit

The Quiet Power of Consistency

With no savings habit, she waited for the perfect moment. Shifting focus to steady action, she automated small monthly savings. Emotion faded, discipline grew, and she learned that wealth builds silently when consistency matters more than mood or immediate results.

S11

SAVINGS & FINANCIAL SECURITY
SS 02 : Fear of Financial Insecurity

Shloka **18.66**	***sarva-dharmān parityajya mām ekaṁ śharaṇaṁ vraja ahaṁ tvāṁ sarva-pāpebhyo mokṣhayiṣhyāmi mā śhuchaḥ***
Simple Translation	• **Surrender with trust and seek refuge.** • **Do not fear—I will free you from distress.**
Meaning	• **Fear clouds financial judgment.** • **Calm faith supports wise decisions.**
Actions	• **Build a dedicated emergency fund.** • **Continuously improve your financial knowledge.**

12

SAVINGS & FINANCIAL SECURITY
SS 02 : Fear of Financial Insecurity

From Fear to Financial Calm

Haunted by financial insecurity, he chose trust over panic. Building an emergency fund and learning financial basics, his mind steadied. Fear loosened its grip, teaching his that calm preparation and knowledge-based decisions offer far stronger protection than constant worry ever could.

S12

SAVINGS & FINANCIAL SECURITY
SS 03 : Lack of Emergency Fund

Shloka 6.13	*samaṁ kāya-śhiro-grīvaṁ dhārayann achalaṁ sthiraḥ samprekṣhya nāsikāgraṁ svaṁ diśhaśh chānavalokayan*
Simple Translation	• Remain steady and well-balanced. • Maintain stability without distraction.
Meaning	• Financial safety builds confidence. • Stability protects you during uncertainty.
Actions	• Save 3–6 months of living expenses. • Keep the amount in easily accessible form.

13

SAVINGS & FINANCIAL SECURITY
SS 03 : Lack of Emergency Fund

Stability Before Uncertainty

Without an emergency fund, every crisis unsettled his mind. Choosing stability, he calmly saved three to six months of expenses in liquid form. Gradually, fear reduced, confidence grew, and he learned that true financial peace begins with preparation that anchors the mind in uncertain times.

S13

SAVINGS & FINANCIAL SECURITY
SS 04 : Lack of Retirement Planning

Shloka **2.14**	***mātrā-sparśhās tu kaunteya*** ***śhītoṣhṇa-sukha-duḥkha-dāḥ*** ***āgamāpāyino 'nityās tans-*** ***titikṣhasva bhārata***
Simple Translation	• **Situations change with time.** • **Prepare yourself with patience.**
Meaning	• **The future will bring change.** • **Early planning ensures security.**
Actions	• **Begin long-term retirement investments early.** • **Increase contributions consistently each year.**

14

SAVINGS & FINANCIAL SECURITY
SS 04 : Lack of Retirement Planning

Preparing for Tomorrow with Patience

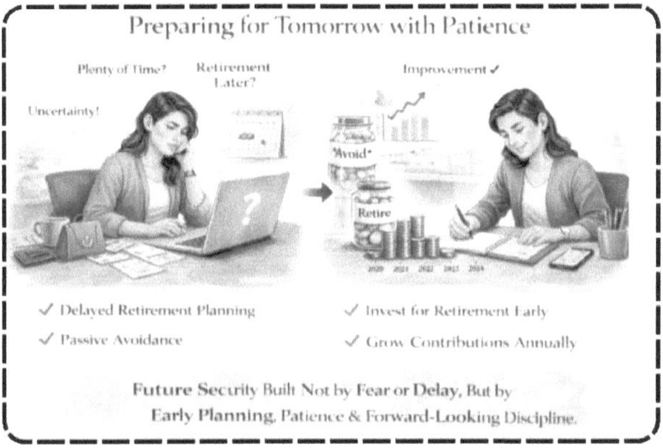

Ignoring retirement felt easy until uncertainty surfaced. Accepting that life constantly changes, she began long-term investments and increased contributions yearly. Calm preparation replaced avoidance, teaching her that future security is not built by fear or delay, but by early planning, patience, and steady, forward-looking discipline.

S14

SAVINGS & FINANCIAL SECURITY
SS 05 : Lack of Insurance

Shloka 2.23	***nainaṁ chhindanti śhastrāṇi nainaṁ dahati pāvakaḥ na chainaṁ kledayantyāpo na śhoṣhayati mārutaḥ***
Simple Translation	• **The true Self cannot be harmed.** • **It remains untouched by external forces.**
Meaning	• **While the soul is eternal, life is uncertain.** • **Practical protection safeguards your family.**
Actions	• **Purchase adequate term life insurance.** • **Secure comprehensive health insurance coverage.**

15

SAVINGS & FINANCIAL SECURITY
SS 05 : Lack of Insurance

Shielding What Matters Most

Ignoring insurance, he lived with hidden anxiety. Realizing protection sustains life's stability, he secured term and health coverage. Relief followed. He learned that caring for family means preparing wisely, and true peace arises when responsibility safeguards loved ones against life's uncertainties.

S15

SAVINGS & FINANCIAL SECURITY
SS 06 : Underestimating Retirement Expenses

Shloka 2.14	***mātrā-sparśhās tu kaunteya śhītoṣhṇa-sukha-duḥkha-dāḥ āgamāpāyino 'nityās tans-titikṣhasva bhārata***
Simple Translation	• **Conditions change with time.** • **Prepare yourself with patience**
Meaning	• **Future expenses will rise.** • **Early retirement planning prevents regret.**
Actions	• **Increase your SIP contributions every year.** • **Factor inflation into long-term planning.**

16

SAVINGS & FINANCIAL SECURITY
SS 06 : Underestimating Retirement Expenses

Preparing for Life's Long Horizon

Underestimating retirement costs, she lived comfortably in the present. Accepting inevitable future changes, she increased SIPs yearly and planned for inflation. Awareness replaced complacency, teaching her that dignified aging is secured not by hope, but by early preparation and steady, foresighted action.

S16

SAVINGS & FINANCIAL SECURITY
SS 07 : Inadequate Medical Insurance

Shloka 6.13	***samaṁ kāya-śhiro-grīvaṁ dhārayann achalaṁ sthiraḥ samprekṣhya nāsikāgraṁ svaṁ diśhaśh chānavalokayan***
Simple Translation	• **Remain steady and well-prepared.** • **Maintain stability with awareness.**
Meaning	• **Health risks are unpredictable.** • **Adequate insurance ensures financial protection.**
Actions	• **Purchase sufficient health insurance coverage.** • **Add necessary riders for comprehensive protection.**

17

SAVINGS & FINANCIAL SECURITY
SS 07 : Inadequate Medical Insurance

Preparedness Brings Peace

Ignoring medical insurance, he lived with hidden vulnerability. Choosing wise preparation, he secured adequate health coverage with necessary riders. Anxiety eased, clarity returned, and he learned that true stability comes not from luck, but from foresight that protects health, finances, and family dignity together.

S17

SAVINGS & FINANCIAL SECURITY
SS 08 : No Protection for Dependents

Shloka 2.23	*nainaṁ chhindanti śhastrāṇi* *nainaṁ dahati pāvakaḥ* *na chainaṁ kledayantyāpo* *na śhoṣhayati mārutaḥ*
Simple Translation	• The true Self cannot be harmed. • It remains untouched by external forces.
Meaning	• While life is uncertain, responsibility remains. • Family security requires practical protection.
Actions	• Purchase adequate term life insurance. • Build a strong emergency fund.

18

SAVINGS & FINANCIAL SECURITY
SS 08 : No Protection for Dependents

Securing Those Who Depend on You

Ignoring protection, he lived with silent worry about his family. Choosing responsibility, he bought term insurance and built an emergency fund. Peace followed, teaching him that true care is not spoken, but shown through foresight that shields loved ones from life's uncertainties.

S18

SAVINGS & FINANCIAL SECURITY
SS 09 : Overdependence on Single Income

Shloka 3.27	***prakṛiteḥ kriyamāṇāni guṇaiḥ karmāṇi sarvaśhaḥ ahankāra-vimūḍhātmā kartāham iti manyate***
Simple Translation	• **All actions arise from nature's forces.** • **Do not assume control rests in one source.**
Meaning	• **Depending on one income increases risk.** • **Diversified effort creates stability.**
Actions	• **Develop at least one additional income stream.** • **Learn skills that can be monetized.**

19

SAVINGS & FINANCIAL SECURITY
SS 09 : Overdependence on Single Income

Strength in Multiple Streams

Relying on a single income, he felt fragile despite hard work. Understanding that effort must diversify, he built a side income and learned monetizable skills. Security slowly strengthened, teaching him that resilience grows when livelihood flows from multiple sources, not ego-bound dependence on one stream alone.

S19

SAVINGS & FINANCIAL SECURITY
SS 10 : Inability to Save for Goals

Shloka 3.19	***tasmād asaktaḥ satataṁ kāryaṁ karma samāchara asakto hyācharan karma param āpnoti pūruṣhaḥ***
Simple Translation	• **Perform your duty with steady dedication.** • **Consistent effort leads to higher success.**
Meaning	• **Financial goals demand discipline.** • **Regular contributions create results.**
Actions	• **Adopt goal-based investing strategies.** • **Prioritize essential goals first.**

20

SAVINGS & FINANCIAL SECURITY
SS 10 : Inability to Save for Goals

Steady Steps Toward Financial Goals

Unable to save for goals, he stopped chasing quick wins and chose steady effort. Using goal-based investing and prioritizing essential needs, consistency took root. Over time, discipline matured into progress, teaching him that financial excellence is achieved not through intensity, but through patient, unwavering commitment.

S20

DEBT & LIABILITY MANAGEMENT
DM 01 : Debt Burden

Shloka 6.5	***uddhared ātmanātmānaṁ nātmānam avasādayet ātmaiva hyātmano bandhur ātmaiva ripur ātmanaḥ***
Simple Translation	• **Lift yourself by your own effort.** • **You are your own friend—or your own obstacle.**
Meaning	• **Freedom begins with self-discipline.** • **Consistent effort reduces financial burden.**
Actions	• **Prepare a structured debt repayment plan.** • **Avoid taking on new unnecessary debt.**

21

DEBT & LIABILITY MANAGEMENT
DM 01 : Debt Burden

Rising Above Debt

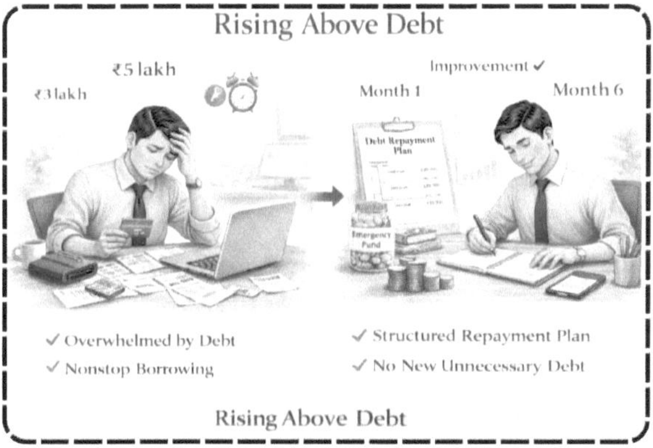

Crushed by debt, he stopped blaming circumstances and chose self-effort. Creating a clear repayment plan and resisting new borrowing, discipline replaced despair. Step by step, control returned, teaching him that financial freedom begins when one lifts oneself through responsibility, patience, and consistent, conscious choices.

S21

DEBT & LIABILITY MANAGEMENT
DM 02 : Compulsive Borrowing

Shloka 6.5	***uddhared ātmanātmānaṁ*** ***nātmānam avasādayet*** ***ātmaiva hyātmano bandhur*** ***ātmaiva ripur ātmanaḥ***
Simple Translation	• **Lift yourself; do not let yourself fall.** • **You are your own friend—and your own enemy.**
Meaning	• **Uncontrolled borrowing weakens freedom.** • **Self-discipline restores financial strength.**
Actions	• **Stop taking new unnecessary loans.** • **Follow a strict and structured repayment plan.**

22

DEBT & LIABILITY MANAGEMENT
DM 02 : Compulsive Borrowing

Breaking the Borrowing Cycle

Trapped in compulsive borrowing, he realized dependence was degrading his dignity. Choosing self-upliftment, he stopped new loans and followed strict repayment discipline. Gradually, control returned, teaching him that financial freedom begins when responsibility replaces escape and self-respect guides every monetary decision.

S22

DEBT & LIABILITY MANAGEMENT
DM 03 : Not Prioritizing Debt Repayment

Shloka 3.8	***niyataṁ kuru karma tvaṁ karma jyāyo hyakarmaṇaḥ śharīra-yātrāpi cha te na prasiddhyed akarmaṇaḥ***
Simple Translation	• **Perform your necessary duties.** • **Action is better than avoidance.**
Meaning	• **Debt repayment cannot be postponed.** • **Responsibility brings financial relief.**
Actions	• **Create a clear repayment schedule.** • **Clear high-interest loans first.**

23

DEBT & LIABILITY MANAGEMENT
DM 03 : Not Prioritizing Debt Repayment

Facing Obligations First

Avoiding debt repayment, he delayed the uncomfortable. Accepting duty over denial, he created a clear repayment schedule and targeted high-interest loans first. Momentum followed action, teaching him that financial relief begins when responsibilities are faced directly and disciplined effort replaces postponement.

S23

DEBT & LIABILITY MANAGEMENT
DM 04 : Heavy EMIs Causing Stress

Shloka 2.48	***yoga-sthaḥ kuru karmāṇi saṅgaṁ tyaktvā dhanañjaya siddhy-asiddhyoḥ samo bhūtvā samatvaṁ yoga uchyate***
Simple Translation	• **Perform your duties with inner balance.** • **Remain steady in success and difficulty.**
Meaning	• **Financial pressure needs calm response.** • **Gradual reduction brings peace.**
Actions	• **Consider refinancing or partial prepayment.** • **Reduce non-essential expenses to ease burden.**

24

DEBT & LIABILITY MANAGEMENT
DM 04 : Restoring Balance Amid Obligations

Restoring Balance Amid Obligations

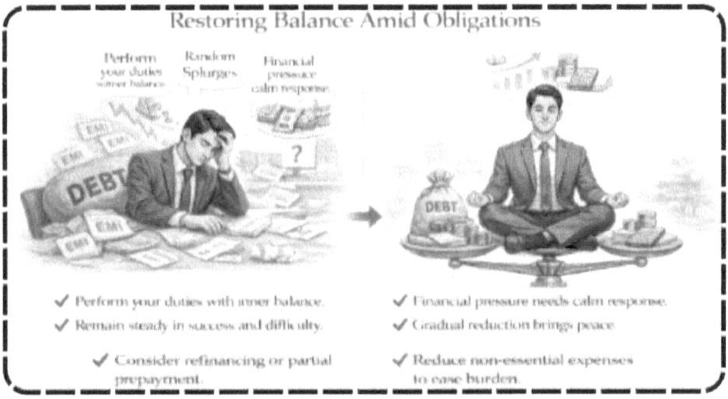

Crushed by heavy EMIs, he learned to stay balanced instead of panicking. Refinancing loans, prepaying gradually, and cutting non-essential expenses eased pressure. Calm action replaced anxiety, teaching him that financial balance returns not through sudden escape, but through patient adjustment and steady discipline.

S24

DEBT & LIABILITY MANAGEMENT
DM 05 : Unnecessary Loans for Lifestyle

Shloka 6.5	*uddhared ātmanātmānaṁ* *nātmānam avasādayet* *ātmaiva hyātmano bandhur* *ātmaiva ripur ātmanaḥ*
Simple Translation	• Lift yourself; do not let yourself fall. • You are your own friend—and your own enemy.
Meaning	• Status-driven debt weakens freedom. • Wise choices protect financial dignity.
Actions	• Reassess non-essential purchases carefully. • Adopt a savings-first approach before spending.

25

DEBT & LIABILITY MANAGEMENT
DM 05 : Unnecessary Loans for Lifestyle

Dignity Over Display

Chasing status, he took unnecessary lifestyle loans and felt trapped. Choosing self-upliftment, he re-evaluated purchases and adopted a savings-first mindset. Freedom slowly returned, teaching him that dignity and peace arise when financial choices honor self-respect rather than external appearances.

S25

DEBT & LIABILITY MANAGEMENT
DM 06 : Not Planning Children's Education Expenses

Shloka **18.78**	***yatra yogeśhvaraḥ kṛiṣhṇo yatra pārtho dhanur-dharaḥ tatra śhrīr vijayo bhūtir dhruvā nītir matir mama***
Simple Translation	• **Where wisdom and disciplined action unite.** • **There arise prosperity and lasting success.**
Meaning	• **Future security requires early discipline.** • **Planned effort today ensures tomorrow's stability.**
Actions	• **Start a dedicated child education SIP early.** • **Increase contributions yearly to match inflation.**

26

DEBT & LIABILITY MANAGEMENT
DM 06 : Not Planning Children's Education Expenses

Securing Tomorrow Through Today's Discipline

Ignoring future education costs, he relied on hope instead of planning. Choosing discipline and foresight, he started a child education SIP and increased it yearly with inflation. Calm replaced worry, teaching him that children's security is built through early, righteous action and consistent preparation.

S26

DEBT & LIABILITY MANAGEMENT
DM 07 : Financial Arguments at Home

Shloka 17.15	***anudvega-karaṁ vākyaṁ satyaṁ priya-hitaṁ cha yat svādhyāyābhyasanaṁ chaiva vāṅ-mayaṁ tapa uchyate***
Simple Translation	• **Speak words that do not cause disturbance.** • **Let them be truthful, kind, and beneficial.**
Meaning	• **Money discussions need calmness.** • **Respectful dialogue prevents conflict.**
Actions	• **Schedule monthly financial discussions.** • **Define and review shared financial goals.**

27

DEBT & LIABILITY MANAGEMENT DM 07 : Financial Arguments at Home

Peaceful Conversations, Shared Prosperity

Money discussions often turned into conflict at home. Choosing gentle, truthful speech, they began calm monthly money meetings. Setting shared goals together, tension eased, trust grew, and they learned that financial harmony is built not by winning arguments, but by respectful dialogue and collective purpose.

S27

DEBT & LIABILITY MANAGEMENT
DM 08 : Financial Stress Causing Family Issues

Shloka 17.15	*anudvega-karaṁ vākyaṁ satyaṁ priya-hitaṁ cha yat svādhyāyābhyasanaṁ chaiva vāṅ-mayaṁ tapa uchyate*
Simple Translation	• Speak words that do not cause distress. • Let them be truthful, kind, and beneficial.
Meaning	• Money stress needs calm communication. • Harmony grows through respectful dialogue
Actions	• Hold structured monthly finance discussions. • Work together to design practical solutions.

28

DEBT & LIABILITY MANAGEMENT
DM 08 : Financial Stress Causing Family Issues

Harmony Through Honest Conversation

Financial stress strained family bonds and fueled arguments. Choosing gentle, truthful speech, they began calm monthly finance meetings. Working jointly on solutions, trust returned, teaching them that harmony at home is restored when money is discussed with patience, respect, and shared responsibility.

S28

DEBT & LIABILITY MANAGEMENT

DM 09 : Emotional Spending During Stress

Shloka 17.15	***krodhād bhavati sammohaḥ sammohāt smṛiti-vibhramaḥ smṛiti-bhranśhād buddhi-nāśho buddhi-nāśhāt praṇaśhyati***
Simple Translation	• **From intense emotion comes confusion.** • **From confusion, judgment is lost.**
Meaning	• **Emotional decisions weaken financial stability.** • **Clarity protects long-term wealth.**
Actions	• **Pause before making non-essential purchases.** • **Redirect stress into healthy activities.**

29

DEBT & LIABILITY MANAGEMENT
DM 09 : Emotional Spending During Stress

Choosing Calm Over Impulse

Stressed and overwhelmed, she shopped to soothe emotions. Remembering how desire clouds judgment, she paused before buying and redirected stress into healthier activities. Awareness replaced impulse, teaching her that emotional balance protects finances better than momentary comfort ever could.

S29

DEBT & LIABILITY MANAGEMENT
DM 10 : Bad Financial Habits

Shloka 3.39	***āvṛitaṁ jñānam etena jñānino nitya-vairiṇā kāma-rūpeṇa kaunteya duṣhpūreṇānalena cha***
Simple Translation	• **Desire covers true wisdom.** • **It burns like an endless fire.**
Meaning	• **Uncontrolled wants weaken judgment.** • **Self-control protects financial health.**
Actions	• **Replace impulsive habits with planned spending.** • **Review and correct habits monthly.**

30

DEBT & LIABILITY MANAGEMENT
DM 10 : Bad Financial Habits

Clearing the Fog of Desire

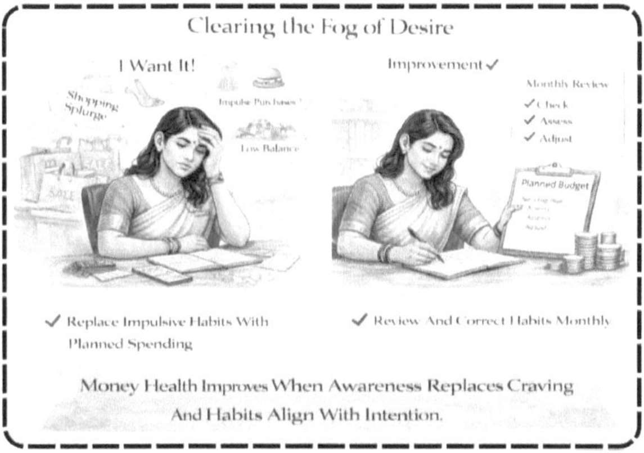

Bad financial habits quietly drained her resources. Recognizing desire as the enemy of wisdom, she replaced impulse spending with planned choices. Reviewing expenses monthly, clarity returned, teaching her that money health improves when awareness replaces craving and habits align with intention.

S30

INVESTMENT & BEHAVIOR
IB 01 : Lack of Investment Knowledge

Shloka 4.38	*na hi jñānena sadṛiśhaṁ* *pavitramiha vidyate* *tatsvayaṁ yogasansiddhaḥ* *kālenātmani vindati*
Simple Translation	• Nothing is as purifying as knowledge. • In time, wisdom reveals itself within.
Meaning	• Financial clarity comes through learning. • Knowledge builds confidence in investing.
Actions	• Study basic investment principles regularly. • Start with simple and relatively safe options.

31

INVESTMENT & BEHAVIOR
IB 01 : Lack of Investment Knowledge

Purified by Financial Knowledge

Intimidated by investing, she avoided decisions and stayed stagnant. Choosing learning as purification, she studied basic concepts and began with safe options. Fear softened into confidence, teaching her that financial growth starts not with risk, but with understanding patiently applied over time.

S31

INVESTMENT & BEHAVIOR
IB 02 : Delayed Investing

Shloka 3.21	***yad yad ācharati śhreṣhṭhas tat tad evetaro janaḥ sa yat pramāṇaṁ kurute lokas tad anuvartate***
Simple Translation	• **What the wise practice, others follow.** • **Your actions set the standard.**
Meaning	• **Delay reduces long-term growth.** • **Start early and lead by example—even for yourself.**
Actions	• **Begin a SIP without postponing.** • **Increase the investment amount every year.**

32

INVESTMENT & BEHAVIOR
IB 02 : Delayed Investing

The Wisdom of Beginning Now

Delaying investment, he kept waiting for the perfect moment. Remembering that the wise lead through action, he began a simple SIP immediately. As discipline formed and contributions grew annually, he learned that starting early sets an example for the future self and quietly builds lasting wealth.

S32

INVESTMENT & BEHAVIOR
IB 03 : Fear of Losing Money

Shloka 2.38	***sukha-duḥkhe same kṛitvā lābhālābhau jayājayau tato yuddhāya yujyasva naivaṁ pāpam avāpsyasi***
Simple Translation	• **Remain steady in gain and loss.** • **Act with balance and courage.**
Meaning	• **Fear disturbs financial judgment.** • **Calm thinking supports better decisions.**
Actions	• **Diversify your investments wisely.** • **Stay committed to a long-term strategy.**

33

INVESTMENT & BEHAVIOR
IB 03 : Fear of Losing Money

Steadiness Amid Market Waves

Fear of loss kept him frozen. Learning to remain steady in gain and loss, he diversified investments and committed to a long-term strategy. Anxiety eased, clarity returned, and he discovered that calm consistency, not emotional reaction, protects wealth through inevitable market ups and downs.

S33

INVESTMENT & BEHAVIOR
IB 04 : Unsure Where to Invest

Shloka 4.34	***tad viddhi praṇipātena paripraśhnena sevayā upadekṣhyanti te jñānaṁ jñāninas tattva-darśhinaḥ***
Simple Translation	• **Approach the wise with humility.** • **Seek knowledge through sincere questions.**
Meaning	• **Guidance prevents costly mistakes.** • **Informed decisions build confidence.**
Actions	• **Consult a qualified financial advisor.** • **Assess and understand your risk profile.**

34

INVESTMENT & BEHAVIOR
IB 04 : Unsure Where to Invest

Guided by Wisdom

Unsure where to invest, she resisted guesswork. Approaching wise advisors with humility, she understood her risk profile and options. Confusion dissolved into clarity, teaching her that sound investing begins not with bold moves, but with guided learning, thoughtful questions, and respect for experienced insight.

S34

INVESTMENT & BEHAVIOR
IB 05 : Fear of Stock Market

Shloka 2.47	***karmaṇy-evādhikāras te mā phaleṣhu kadāchana mā karma-phala-hetur bhūr mā te saṅgo 'stvakarmaṇi***
Simple Translation	• **You have control over your actions.** • **Do not be attached to short-term results.**
Meaning	• **Fear reduces with long-term perspective.** • **Consistency builds investing confidence.**
Actions	• **Begin with small SIP investments.** • **Learn basic principles of equity investing.**

35

INVESTMENT & BEHAVIOR
IB 05 : Fear of Stock Market

Courage Through Consistent Action

Fear of the stock market kept her inactive and doubtful. Shifting focus from results to action, she began small SIPs and learned equity basics. Gradually, understanding replaced fear, teaching her that long-term discipline and steady learning transform uncertainty into confidence and purposeful financial growth.

S35

INVESTMENT & BEHAVIOR
IB 06 : Investing Based on Emotions

Shloka 2.56	***duḥkheṣhv-anudvigna-manāḥ sukheṣhu vigata-spṛihaḥ vīta-rāga-bhaya-krodhaḥ sthita-dhīr munir uchyate***
Simple Translation	• **One who is undisturbed in sorrow, And free from fear or excitement is steady.**
Meaning	• **Emotional reactions distort investing decisions.** • **Calm discipline protects long-term wealth.**
Actions	• **Invest according to a clear written plan.** • **Stay committed to long-term financial goals.**

36

INVESTMENT & BEHAVIOR
IB 06 : Investing Based on Emotions

Wisdom Beyond Market Emotions

Swept by fear in losses and excitement in gains, he kept changing investments. Learning steadiness, he committed to a clear plan and long-term goals. Calm replaced reaction, teaching him that wealth grows when decisions arise from balance, patience, and disciplined detachment, not emotional swings.

S36

INVESTMENT & BEHAVIOR

IB 07 : Not Diversifying Investments

Shloka 3.27	***prakṛiteḥ kriyamāṇāni guṇaiḥ karmāṇi sarvaśhaḥ ahankāra-vimūḍhātmā kartāham iti manyate***
Simple Translation	• **All actions arise from nature's forces.** • **Do not assume control lies in one source.**
Meaning	• **Relying on one asset increases risk.** • **Diversification builds financial stability.**
Actions	• **Allocate investments across multiple asset classes.** • **Avoid overexposure to a single instrument.**

37

INVESTMENT & BEHAVIOR
IB 07 : Not Diversifying Investments

Strength in Diversification

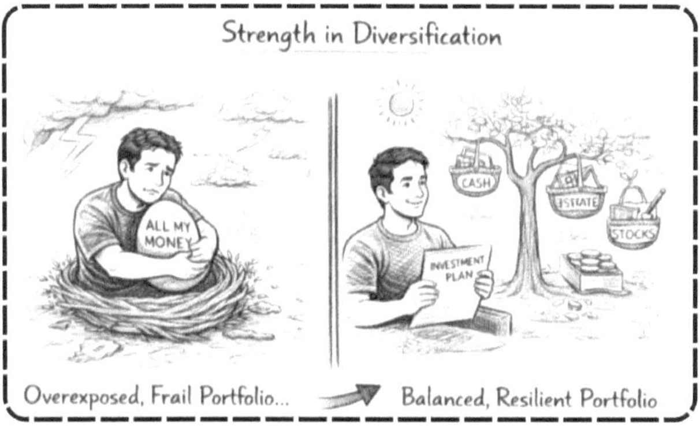

Relying on one investment, he believed control ensured safety. Understanding that outcomes arise beyond ego, he diversified across assets. Risk softened, stability improved, and he learned that financial strength grows not from concentration alone, but from thoughtful spread and respect for uncertainty.

S37

INVESTMENT & BEHAVIOR
IB 08 : Selling Investments Too Early

Shloka 2.38	*sukha-duḥkhe same kṛitvā* *lābhālābhau jayājayau* *tato yuddhāya yujyasva naivaṁ* *pāpam avāpsyasi*
Simple Translation	• **Be steady in gain and loss.** • **Act with balance and courage.**
Meaning	• **Impatience reduces long-term returns.** • **Patience allows compounding to work.**
Actions	• **Commit to a defined long-term horizon.** • **Avoid reacting to short-term market fluctuations.**

38

INVESTMENT & BEHAVIOR
IB 08 : Selling Investments Too Early

Patience Builds Wealth

Fearful of short-term losses, he sold investments too early. Learning to remain equal in gain and loss, he stayed invested through market dips. Patience rewarded him, teaching that wealth grows steadily when calm conviction replaces panic and time is allowed to work its quiet magic.

S38

INVESTMENT & BEHAVIOR
IB 09 : Buying Assets Without Research

Shloka 4.34	***tad viddhi praṇipātena paripraśhnena sevayā upadekṣhyanti te jñānaṁ jñāninas tattva-darśhinaḥ***
Simple Translation	• **Approach the wise with humility.** • **Gain knowledge through sincere inquiry.**
Meaning	• **Major purchases require careful study.** • **Informed decisions reduce costly mistakes.**
Actions	• **Evaluate risks and long-term impact.** • **Consult qualified financial professionals before investing.**

39

INVESTMENT & BEHAVIOR
IB 09 :Buying Assets Without Research

Wisdom Before Wealth

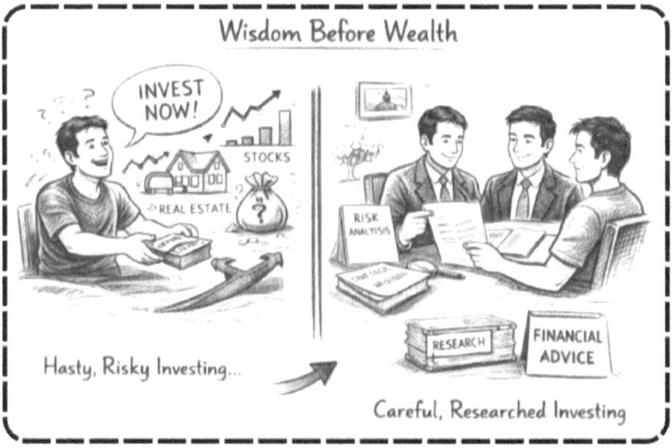

Eager to invest, he once bought assets without understanding risks. Learning humility, he researched carefully and consulted financial professionals. Clarity replaced haste, teaching him that major financial decisions prosper when guided by knowledge, patience, and respect for experienced wisdom rather than impulsive confidence.

S39

INVESTMENT & BEHAVIOR
IB 10 : Blindly Trusting Financial Agents

Shloka 4.34	*tad viddhi praṇipātena paripraśhnena sevayā upadekṣhyanti te jñānaṁ jñāninas tattva-darśhinaḥ*
Simple Translation	• Approach with humility and sincere questions. • Gain knowledge through thoughtful inquiry.
Meaning	• Trust should be supported by understanding. • Informed clients make safer decisions.
Actions	• Cross-check all recommendations independently. • Read and understand documents before signing.

40

INVESTMENT & BEHAVIOR
IB 10 :Blindly Trusting Financial Agents

Trust Anchored in Awareness

Blind trust once led him into poor financial choices. Choosing humility and inquiry, he began questioning recommendations and reading documents carefully. Understanding replaced dependence, teaching him that true trust is strengthened by verification, and financial safety grows when learning walks alongside advice.

S40

WEALTH CREATION
WC 01 : Poor Record-Keeping

Shloka 4.39	*śhraddhāvān labhate jñānaṁ* *tat-paraḥ sanyatendriyaḥ* *jñānaṁ labdhvā parāṁ śhāntim* *achireṇādhigachchhati*
Simple Translation	• The disciplined and sincere gain knowledge. • With knowledge comes lasting clarity.
Meaning	• Order brings financial peace. • Clear records prevent confusion.
Actions	• Maintain a simple financial tracking system. • Review and organize documents every month.

41

WEALTH CREATION
WC 01 : Poor Record-Keeping

Order Brings Peace

Poor record-keeping left her anxious and uncertain. Choosing discipline, she maintained a financial tracker and organized documents monthly. Gradually, clarity emerged, stress reduced, and she learned that faith expressed through orderly habits brings knowledge, control, and lasting peace in financial life.

S41

WEALTH CREATION
WC 02 : Lack of Financial Goals

Shloka 18.63	***iti te jñānam ākhyātaṁ guhyād guhyataraṁ mayā vimṛiśhyaitad aśheṣheṇa yathechchhasi tathā kuru***
Simple Translation	• **I have shared this wisdom with you.** • **Reflect deeply, then choose your path.**
Meaning	• **Money without direction gets wasted.** • **Clear goals guide purposeful spending and investing.**
Actions	• **Define short-, medium-, and long-term goals.** • **Allocate funds systematically toward each goal.**

42

WEALTH CREATION
WC 02 : Lack of Financial Goals

Choosing a Financial Direction

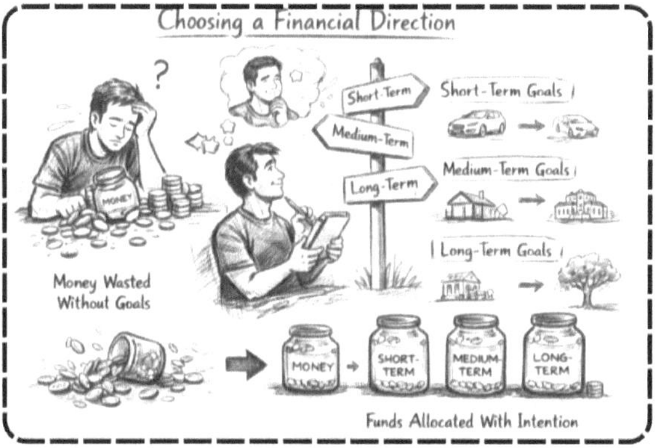

Without financial goals, his money slipped away unnoticed. Pausing to reflect, he defined short, medium, and long-term aims. Allocating funds with intention, clarity replaced confusion, teaching him that wealth grows purposefully only when direction is chosen thoughtfully, not left to chance.

S42

WEALTH CREATION
WC 03 : Not Reviewing Financial Plan

Shloka 4.7	***yadā yadā hi dharmasya glānir bhavati bhārata abhyutthānam adharmasya tadātmānaṁ sṛijāmyaham***
Simple Translation	• **Whenever imbalance arises, Restoration begins at the right time.**
Meaning	• **Plans need periodic correction.** • **Review prevents long-term deviation.**
Actions	• **Conduct a half-yearly financial review.** • **Adjust goals, SIPs, and allocations accordingly.**

43

WEALTH CREATION
WC 03 : Not Reviewing Financial Plan

Course Correction Through Review

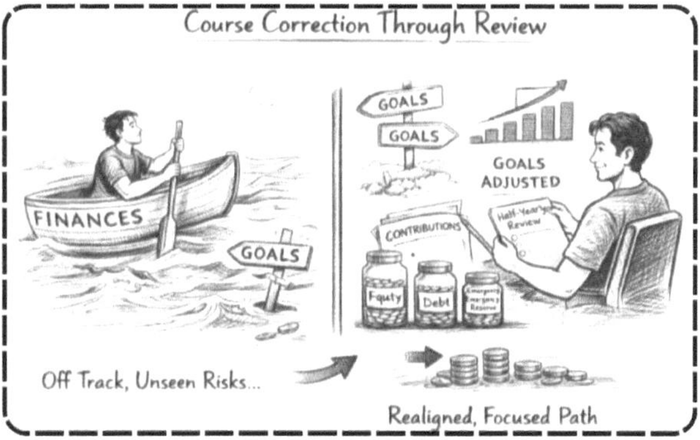

Neglecting financial reviews, he drifted off track without noticing. Choosing timely reflection, he conducted half-yearly reviews and adjusted goals and contributions. Corrections emerged naturally, teaching him that solutions appear when awareness returns and disciplined review realigns effort with evolving needs.

S43

WEALTH CREATION
WC 04 : Falling for Scams

Shloka 4.38	***na hi jñānena sadṛiśhaṁ pavitramiha vidyate tatsvayaṁ yogasansiddhaḥ kālenātmani vindati***
Simple Translation	• **Nothing is as purifying as knowledge.** • **With time, wisdom protects the seeker.**
Meaning	• **Ignorance invites financial deception.** • **Awareness safeguards your wealth.**
Actions	• **Verify credentials and details before investing.** • **Avoid schemes promising unrealistic returns.**

44

WEALTH CREATION
WC 04 : Falling for Scams

Protection Through Awareness

After falling for scams, he replaced embarrassment with learning. Studying basics and verifying every offer, he avoided unrealistic promises. Knowledge sharpened judgment, teaching him that financial safety grows not from blind trust, but from informed caution and patient, conscious decision-making.

S44

WEALTH CREATION
WC 05 : Depending on Luck Instead of Planning

Shloka 3.21	***yad yad ācharati śhreṣhṭhas tat tad evetaro janaḥ sa yat pramāṇaṁ kurute lokas tad anuvartate***
Simple Translation	• **What the wise practice, others follow.** • **Actions set the standard for results.**
Meaning	• **Success comes from disciplined action.** • **Planning replaces dependence on luck.**
Actions	• **Define clear financial goals.** • **Execute structured and consistent financial steps.**

45

WEALTH CREATION
WC 05 : Depending on Luck Instead of Planning

Designing Fortune Through Action

Relying on luck, he drifted financially without direction. Learning that success is created, not wished for, he set clear goals and followed structured actions. Gradually, control replaced hope, teaching him that consistent planning and disciplined effort shape destiny far more reliably than chance ever can.

S45

WEALTH CREATION
WC 06 : No Wealth Creation Plan

Shloka 3.19	*tasmād asaktaḥ satataṁ kāryaṁ karma samāchara asakto hyācharan karma param āpnoti pūruṣhaḥ*
Simple Translation	• Perform your duty with steady dedication. • Consistent effort leads to higher success.
Meaning	• Wealth grows through disciplined action. • Consistency builds long-term prosperity.
Actions	• Invest a fixed amount every month. • Increase your SIP contribution annually.

46

WEALTH CREATION
WC 06 : No Wealth Creation Plan

Building Wealth Through Steady Commitment

Without a wealth plan, he drifted between intentions and inaction. Choosing dedication over delay, he began monthly investing and increased SIPs yearly. Consistency replaced confusion, teaching him that true wealth is created not by sudden moves, but by disciplined effort repeated patiently over time.

S46

WEALTH CREATION
WC 07 : Poor Tax Filing Habits

Shloka 4.42	*tasmād ajñāna-sambhūtaṁ hṛit-sthaṁ jñānāsinātmanaḥ chhittvainaṁ sanśhayaṁ yogam ātiṣhṭhottiṣhṭha bhārata*
Simple Translation	• Cut ignorance with the sword of knowledge. • Rise with clarity and firm action.
Meaning	• Delay in tax matters creates stress. • Timely compliance ensures peace of mind.
Actions	• Maintain organized financial documents. • File taxes well before the due date.

47

WEALTH CREATION
WC 07 : Poor Tax Filing Habits

Clarity Through Timely Compliance

Poor tax habits bred anxiety and confusion. Choosing knowledge over neglect, he organized documents and filed taxes on time. Doubt dissolved into confidence, teaching him that financial peace is preserved when ignorance is cut away through awareness, preparation, and disciplined, timely action.

S47

WEALTH CREATION
WC 08 : Emotional Reaction to Market Volatility

Shloka 2.14	***mātrā-sparśhās tu kaunteya śhītoṣhṇa-sukha-duḥkha-dāḥ āgamāpāyino 'nityās tans-titikṣhasva bhārata***
Simple Translation	• **Pleasure and pain come and go.** • **They are temporary—learn to endure.**
Meaning	• **Market ups and downs are natural.** • **Calm patience protects long-term returns.**
Actions	• **Adhere to your planned asset allocation.** • **Avoid panic selling during volatility.**

48

WEALTH CREATION
WC 08 : Emotional Reaction to Market Volatility

Calm Through Market Cycles

Market swings triggered fear and excitement within him. Remembering that ups and downs are temporary, he stuck to his asset allocation and avoided panic selling. Calm endurance replaced reaction, teaching him that wealth survives volatility when patience, discipline, and long-term perspective steady the mind.

S48

WEALTH CREATION
WC 09 : Following Others' Financial Habits Blindly

Shloka 3.35	*śhreyān swa-dharmo viguṇaḥ para-dharmāt sv-anuṣhṭhitāt swa-dharme nidhanaṁ śhreyaḥ para-dharmo bhayāvahaḥ*
Simple Translation	• Better to follow your own path, even imperfectly. • Another's path may lead to fear.
Meaning	• Financial planning must suit your life. • Blind imitation creates risk.
Actions	• Evaluate your personal goals and needs. • Design a strategy instead of copying others.

49

WEALTH CREATION
WC 09 : Following Others' Financial Habits Blindly

Walking Your Financial Path

Copying others' financial habits left him confused and anxious. Reflecting on his own goals, he designed a plan suited to his life. Peace returned, teaching him that financial security grows when one follows a personal path, not borrowed strategies driven by comparison or fear.

S49

WEALTH CREATION
WC 10 : Not Planning for Inflation

Shloka 4.43	***śhreyān dravya-mayād yajñāj jñāna-yajñaḥ parantapa sarvaṁ karmākhilaṁ pārtha jñāne parisamāpyate***
Simple Translation	• **Knowledge-guided action is superior.** • **Wisdom brings clarity to every decision.**
Meaning	• **Costs will rise over time.** • **Planning must account for inflation.**
Actions	• **Allocate funds to inflation-beating assets.** • **Review and adjust your plan annually.**

50

WEALTH CREATION
WC 10 : Not Planning for Inflation

Staying Ahead of Rising Costs

Ignoring inflation, he planned finances on yesterday's numbers. Choosing knowledge-led action, he invested in inflation-beating assets and reviewed plans annually. Awareness replaced complacency, teaching him that long-term security depends on anticipating change and adjusting strategies before rising costs erode hard-earned wealth.

S50

www.ingramcontent.com/pod-product-compliance
Ingram Content Group UK Ltd.
Pitfield, Milton Keynes, MK11 3LW, UK
UKHW040036200726
13845UKWH00054B/412

9 789358 120226